D0344174

HEAVEN
BOUND

Living in the light of eternity

SELWYN HUGHES

HEAVEN BOUND

Living in the light of eternity

CONTENTS

CONTENTS

INTRODUCTION

We are going to be looking at a subject about which comparatively little has been written in our generation – heaven. Our Christian forefathers continually talked and wrote about this topic, but nowadays for some reason the subject is seldom discussed. Can part of the reason be, I wonder, that to show an interest in heaven leaves us open to the charge – even from fellow Christians – of 'otherworldliness'?

During the past few decades there has been such an emphasis on the 'social gospel' that many of us are afraid to talk of heaven in case our belief is thought to be 'pie in the sky'. Well, let it be said right away that the 'social gospel' is not the whole gospel. We must not neglect our responsibilities to the community, the nation and the world, and we must do everything we can to ease the plight of those who are deprived. However, we must never lose sight of the fact that the only 'new Jerusalem' we shall see is not man-made but is eternal and in heaven. Some of the greatest social reformers – John Wesley, Lord Shaftesbury, William Booth, for example – were God-intoxicated men who constantly kept heaven in view. They worked the better down here because by faith they always had the perfect in view.

It is not 'otherwordly' to talk and think about heaven – providing that is not *all* we think about. Thus I make no apology for directing your thoughts towards heaven.

It is, after all, our final destination – the ultimate goal of every believer. Here we sojourn. There we *belong*. Nothing must ever be allowed to make us forget that.

CHAPTER ONE

LONGING FOR HOME

1 Peter 1:1–9;
Ecclesiastes 3:1–14;
Hebrews 9:11–28

*'… an inheritance that can never perish, spoil
or fade – kept in heaven for you …'*
1 Peter 1:4

Does keeping the prospect of heaven ever before us make us less keen to serve our brothers and sisters here below? There is something wrong if that is so. Think of the tremendous social consequences of the work of the men we referred to in the introduction – Wesley, Shaftesbury and Booth. With zest and skill they endeavoured to bring about the outworking of God's purposes on this earth, yet they were completely sure of heaven and talked often about it. As they worked they sang:

> *Strangers and pilgrims here below,*
> *This earth we know is not our place,*
> *But hasten through the vale of woe,*
> *And restless to behold Thy face.*

I contend that you will work the better for God here on earth when, by faith, you have the perfect end in view. So don't run away with the idea that as I guide you through some devotional thinking on the subject of heaven your impact for God here on earth will be lessened. Some in the past have become so preoccupied with heaven that they were then no earthly good, but that need not happen to you. In fact, when you hold the vision of heaven ever before you it will spur you on in your work for God here below as it will be a constant reminder that, no matter how permanent you think things may be, everything is but a tent and at any time the word may come to draw the pegs.

Pilgrims passing through

Over the years I have met some very godly people and one thing that has always impressed me about those who live close to the Lord is that they have about them the 'air of an exile'. This earth, they seem to say both by their actions and their demeanour, is not their place. They are just pilgrims passing through.

I had the privilege once of knowing a man whom I consider the most Christlike person I have ever met. He was a coal miner, and what was astonishing was to see how non-Christians related to him. No one would curse or swear in his presence, and if perchance they forgot themselves and let slip a bad word they would instantly apologise. When he died almost everyone from the coal pit where he had worked attended his funeral. I saw strong men crying like babies as his body was lowered into the grave. One of Wales's most famous preachers gave the funeral address, and although I have forgotten much of what he said I remember a graphic phrase he used when speaking of the miner's life. It is the phrase I used a few moments ago. 'Our brother,' he said, 'had about him the air of an exile.'

The same could have been said, I am sure, of the apostle Paul. How busy he was for the kingdom of God, but he expressed his longing in 2 Corinthians 5:8 to be 'at home with the Lord'. I have come to the conclusion that the more godly people are, the more they will view the things of this world in the same way that they view the furniture in a hotel room. Though it may be tasteful and appealing, it is not all that important. They are not staying. But that fact in no way makes them appear unnatural or disinterested in what is going on around them.

One preacher put this point very effectively when he said: 'If you have spiritual discernment whenever you meet a saint you become aware of two things about him. At one moment you feel how natural and at home he is, and the next you say to yourself: "This man is an exile; he doesn't belong here at all. He is the pilgrim on an inward Odyssey." '

We also referred to the fact that the apostle Paul was busy for the kingdom of God in this world but yet he longed for *home*. And the same could be said of the apostle Peter. In 1 Peter 1:1–9 he reminds his readers of the hope given to every believer of an inheritance that can never perish – *kept in heaven*. I know I am repeating myself but I think the saying bears repetition: the more godly a person is the more aware he or she seems to be of heaven. Contrast this with the statement made by a well-known British author which I once read in a magazine: 'I have no interest in what lies beyond this life. Earth satisfies me. When this life is over, I will have had all that I want of life.' How sad. I certainly have not found all I want in this life. My soul aches for something more satisfying than I have ever discovered on earth. I have had a taste of heaven down here on earth, but it is only a *taste*. The full banquet comes later.

Our home is in God

Ecclesiastes 3:11 suggests that when God designed us He put within us longings for immortality – a yearning for eternity. What has fascinated me over the years is to see how this simple but powerful fact makes itself known in people's lives. Wordsworth, in his 'Intimations of Immortality', put it like this:

> *Our birth is but a sleep and a forgetting,*
> *The soul that rises with us, our life's star,*
> *Hath elsewhere its setting,*
> *And cometh from afar:*
> *Not in entire forgetfulness,*
> *And not in utter nakedness,*
> *But trailing clouds of glory do we come*
> *From God who is our home.*

Note the last line, 'From God who is our home'. Is it this – the fact that we came from God – that accounts for the mysterious homesickness felt by every human heart? I believe it is. We were made by God for God, and there is a restlessness in us that will never go away until we find our home in God. All feel it but not all understand it. A man with whom I chatted once when I was in Malaysia – a good and godly man – said to me, 'Why is it that I never feel at home in this world?'

I answered, 'You were never meant to.' Never.

Hunger of the soul

So, because God has put eternity into the hearts of every one of us we should not be surprised when people start talking about longings for immortality or sensing that they are strangers in this world.

Those with a philosophical bent – the thinkers – seem to get in touch with this fact more easily than those who live just for the moment. Malcolm Muggeridge, who had without doubt an extremely keen mind, said in his book *Jesus Rediscovered* that from the time he was a boy he had the sense of being a stranger in this world and that there was a world beyond this to which he felt he was moving. He wrote, 'I strain my ears to hear the distant music; my eyes to see the bright light far away. The only ultimate disaster that can befall us I have come to realise is to feel ourselves to be at home here on earth. As long as we are aliens we cannot forget our true homeland.'

God has put eternity into the hearts of every one of us.

The Christian message makes this longing for immortality, this hunger of the soul for home, clear to us. And that is why this nostalgia for home is understood aright only by those who have had their hearts illuminated by the gospel. Most men and women in the world don't quite know what is wrong with them. They are aware there are times when they want to be alone, when they look to the calendar or the stars or death to speak to them. They know they long for something. But what? How grateful we should be that what we long for has been made clear to us through the gospel.

Homesickness

We are saying that there is a nostalgia in the heart of every man and women for heaven. Some time ago, in the Bible devotional notes I write, *Every Day with Jesus*, I referred to the fact that the word nostalgia comes from two Greek words: *nostos*, meaning return home, and *algos*, meaning pain. Forgive me for reminding you again. Originally the word meant homesickness because that is an incurable malady, incurable by anything except, of course, home.

On one occasion I heard a Christian psychiatrist say, 'Homesickness is the one common malady of mankind out of which all other problems emerge.' What did he mean? I think he meant this: because God has built into us longings for Himself there is something in all of us which the world cannot satisfy. Money will not satisfy it. Fame will not satisfy it. Pleasure will not satisfy it. Not even a father, mother, spouse or dearest friend can satisfy it.

... the world cannot satisfy.

What we long for in our souls simply cannot be provided by any earthly relationship.

To deny or ignore the longings that God has put

within us for Himself will deaden a part of our souls – the part that aches for Him. This deadness produces such a level of discomfort in the personality that it can be assuaged only by more denial or an attempt to satisfy the ache in ways other than God. To refuse to admit to our spiritual longings is to put the soul in peril. No sense of true security or significance exists in a soul where God is not present. And without true security and significance we are an easy prey for problems.

Further Study

2 Cor.5:1–10; Luke 10:20; Heb. 11:10
1. What did Paul long for?
2. What are we to rejoice in?

Phil. 1:12–26; 1 Thess. 4:13–18
3. What was Paul torn between?
4. What are we to encourage each other with?

John 14:1–7; Heb. 11:16; Phil. 3:20
5. What was the focus of the heroes of faith?
6. What should our focus be?

CHAPTER TWO

MAKING A DETOUR

Isaiah 55:1–13;
Romans 8:1–17;
Jeremiah 17:1–10

*'Why spend money on what is not bread, and
your labour on what does not satisfy'*
Isaiah 55:2

Clearly, most people, if they only allow themselves to feel it, experience the sensation of not being quite at home in this world because something very important awaits us elsewhere. Aldous Huxley said, 'Sooner or later one asks even of Beethoven, even of Shakespeare ... "Is this all?" ' C.S. Lewis described this as 'the inconsolable longing ... news from a country we have never visited.' And you don't need to be a Christian to experience what I am talking about. Augustine spoke about having this perception long before his conversion. C.S. Lewis struggled hard and fought against the idea that the source of his 'inconsolable longing' and the God of traditional religion might be one and the same. Of his search for God Lewis said, 'They might as well talk about the mouse's search for the cat.'

The soul's deep sense of home-lessness.

This prompts a question: If it is true that a longing for heaven has been built into the human heart, how does the great mass of humanity go about dealing with it? One way is to pretend this mysterious aspect of our existence does not exist. It is a strange fact of life that this aspect of human nature – the soul's deep sense of homelessness – is not studied more intently. I wonder why. Perhaps it's because it fits none of the usual categories of thought. It can't be labelled, sorted, explained or matched so men and women make a detour to avoid it and treat it as if it wasn't there. But the detour is really a denial.

None so blind …

Another way, however, is to face the fact that there is an inconsolable longing in the heart but to reduce it to something classifiable and explainable. Human beings have a tendency whenever they are unable to find an explanation for some matter to fit it into a category for which they do have an explanation. This brings it into the sphere of manageability.

Dr Lawrence Crabb, a Christian and a psychologist, frequently stresses this point in his writings. 'Instead of sitting quietly before mystery,' he says, 'we try to bring it into the area of manageability. What fools we are.' When we do this, then it should not surprise us that the phenomenon we are talking about gets a little damaged in the process. William Kirk Kilpatrick, another psychologist, says of such an attempt: 'It is like trying to fit a size twelve shoe into a size four shoebox, or trying to stuff a bird of paradise into a canary cage. Once you cram it in there it won't look like a bird of paradise any more.'

This passion to explain matters is our way of bringing them under our control. We feel less helpless and vulnerable when we are able to manage things than when we have to sit quietly before mystery. But the affairs of the soul cannot always be managed; they are best handled by sitting quietly before God in private prayer.

If you have ever read C.S. Lewis's *The Silver Chair* you will be familiar with the section where the beautiful

Queen of the Underworld tries to convince the children from the Overworld that her dismal kingdom is the only reality and their world is but an imagined dream. 'There is no sun,' she says. 'You have seen my lamps and imagined that there was a sun.' This tactic used by the Queen of the Underworld is practised by many today, especially those who are part of what is called 'the psychological society'. I heard one psychologist say during a television programme: 'The yearnings that we feel inside us can all be explained in terms of our sexuality, and the yearning that Christians say is the yearning for heaven or the homeland they are looking for is nothing more than a desire to return to their mother's womb.' Do you hear the tactic of the Queen of the Underworld? 'You have seen my lamps and imagined that there was a sun.'

Sitting quietly before God in private prayer.

Perhaps in the light of Romans 8 verse 7 we should not blame unbelievers too much for their blindness. But there again, as the saying goes, 'There are none so blind as those who do not wish to see.'

Utopia

Yet another way in which the men and women of the world deal with the fact that there is within their hearts a feeling that something very important awaits us elsewhere is by interpreting it as the desire for Utopia. Are you familiar with the word 'Utopia'? It is not much used nowadays, but when I was growing up it was frequently mentioned. Utopia is an imaginary place with a perfect social and political system, an ideally perfect place or state of things.

In the 1920s and 30s politicians fervently believed they could bring about such a state of perfection. 'With more advanced education,' they said, 'with increased knowledge, better understanding of social forces, we are coming to the point where we should be able to provide healthy, happy and useful lives for all. The day is not far off when no need will have to go unsatisfied and no child go unloved.' Then came World War II, after which we learned that in one of the best educated societies of the day millions of Jews had been gassed. There has not been much talk of Utopia since.

But now and again I hear some befuddled politicians talk about their desire to see the world become a kind of heaven on earth, which could easily be achieved, they believe, 'if we learned to control the variables that affect happiness'. They do not realise that a pleasant and civilised environment is inadequate to deal with the sinful desires of the human heart. Time and time again the attempt to improve conditions has been made and has failed. You can put a pig in a parlour, but you can't put the parlour in a pig.

Just a stopover

No doubt you have heard the sentiment expressed, 'There is no heaven, but this world can be made into a kind of heaven.' To be fair, some who advance this view are quite sincere in their beliefs – politicians in particular – but they are, of course, sincerely wrong. They do not set out to bribe us away from our 'sense of exile'; they are simply misguided. This world is not our final destination. It is just a stopover. However comfortable one may make it, it simply will not satisfy the soul.

Do you remember the fallen angels in Milton's writings who, upon reaching the black burning pit, tried to convince one another that it wasn't such a bad place after all? This is what many men and women do: they try to convince themselves and others that if the ugly parts of life are overlooked then the world can be regarded as a kind of heaven. Looked at from one perspective this world is a beautiful place, but looked at from another, it is a bad place. It is a world of beautiful forests, lakes, mountains, seas, yet within every human heart is a disease called sin which the environment is powerless to eradicate.

William Kirk Kilpatrick made this point: 'The healthy mind works upwards, not downwards. It sees a sun-lamp and thinks of the sun – not the other way around.' Sin desensitises the soul to such a degree that some do not even realise that deep within them is a yearning for eternity. They accept the lower rather than reaching for the higher. They settle for a sun-lamp instead of the sun.

Those who allow themselves to be persuaded that the world is our home, our *only* home, discover, like Alice in Wonderland, that they are growing smaller. And not only do they themselves grow smaller, the world grows smaller too. A world such as this, beautiful though it may be, is not good enough to properly be called home. A waiting place – yes. A dwelling place – yes. But not *home*. Not really.

They settle for a sun-lamp instead of the sun.

To trivialise the built-in desire we have for heaven and eternity has the same effect on the soul as psychotropic drugs have upon the mind: they dull it and deaden it. Far better to listen to the urge deep within us. I contend that there is something in us all that simply refuses to accept that this world is all there is. As soon as we think we have put these built-in longings to sleep they spring up again and cry out for satisfaction. None of the remedies the experts prescribe for dealing with this inner yearning do the trick.

The modern nostrum for dealing with personal discomfort is to 'discover yourself', 'accept yourself', 'get a good self-image'. But those who have discovered their self usually don't like the self they have discovered. How can you accept a sinful self? And those who have discovered themselves and say, 'This is what I have been looking for all my life' know full well that it really isn't what they have been looking for. They settle for something that deep down they know is not what they want to settle for. It's all so sad. So very sad.

Further Study

Psa. 63:1–11; 143:6; 119:174
1. How did the psalmist describe this world?
2. How did he speak for all mankind?

Isa. 59:1–10; Eph. 4:17–19; 1 John 2:11
3. How does Isaiah decribe the result of spiritual blindness?
4. How does Paul describe the Gentiles' thinking?

Matt.15:1–20; Luke 6:43–45; Prov. 4:23
5. Why can't this world be made into a kind of heaven?
6. What are we to guard?

CHAPTER THREE

WE HAVE HIS WORD

Matt. 16:21–28;
John 3:1–16; 8:48–58; 14:1–14

*'In my Father's house are many rooms;
if it were not so I would have told you. I am going
there to prepare a place for you.'*
John 14:2

We turn now to ask ourselves the question: Is the longing for heaven which God has placed within our hearts (though with many it is ignored, modified or denied) enough evidence that there is a heaven? Those with a more scientific mindset will say that subjectivity is not enough. You need more objective proof otherwise you may be deceiving yourself.

A young scientist once put it to me like this: those who have travelled across a desert know the deception of the mirage. A person sees water in front of him. He would bank his life on it being there, but as he reaches out to drink, it fades away. This shows how our human senses are subject to illusions. When we long for something our mind sometimes persuades us that it is available. So how do we know the longing for heaven isn't just a mirage, that it isn't a form of self-delusion? I pointed the young scientist to John 14 verse 2 in which Jesus says, 'I am going there to prepare a place for you.' We have the best proof possible: Jesus has told us there is a heaven and that a place in it is reserved for the men and women who believe in Him. What better evidence do we need than the words of Jesus?

What better evidence do we need than the words of Jesus?

Of course, if a person doesn't believe in Jesus or accept His credibility then that is another matter. Jesus' word is good enough for me, however, and I am sure for most of you who are reading these lines. He has told us in the clearest of terms that He will meet those of us who are His one day in heaven. The One who said, 'I am the truth' has given us His word.

Memories!

The only person ever to have lived in this world and possessed first-hand knowledge of heaven is our Lord Jesus Christ. Suppose someone appeared on our television screens and professed to be able to give us a reliable report of life on some other planet. What would our initial reaction be? Would it not be: How do you know? How can you tell if you have never been there?

In John 8 verse 58 we see quite clearly that Jesus was aware of His pre-existence. But how much did He remember of the glories He left behind? How conscious was He of the life He had lived in heaven? Some say Christ had no remembrance of the splendour He had relinquished. The reason He knew of His pre-existence was because it was revealed to Him by God His Father. Others maintain He had a full and complete memory of His days in heaven.

I think the truth lies somewhere between these two schools of thought. Christ had some memories of heaven but only enough to enable Him to fulfil His redemptive mission. There were certain things He did not know in His human state because He had freely chosen to be ignorant of them, one being the day and hour of the second coming (Matt. 24:36). But He was aware, I believe, to a degree appropriate to His human condition, of the atmosphere, the glory and the delights of heaven. If He had no memories of His pre-existence and what heaven was like how could He have declared, 'If it were not so, I would have told you' (John 14:2)?

Engaging honesty

Let's linger a little longer on the words 'if it were not so, I would have told you' as there is more in them than we might suppose at first glance.

We have accepted that these words indicate Jesus had some remembrance of heaven. How else could He have said, 'If it were not so, I would have told you'? But they reveal something more: they tell us about our Lord's engaging honesty. Can those of us who are Christ's followers believe that He would allow us to labour under a delusion concerning the future life? Do you think He would permit us to put faith in a falsehood? From all that we know of Him we are compelled to say that in every circumstance He would tell us the truth.

Christ was as much a realist as an idealist – He never pretended that things were other than they were. Look at how He dealt with the man who said, somewhat enthusiastically, 'I will follow you wherever you go' (Matt. 8:19). Christ's reply was chilly in its realism, 'Foxes have holes and birds ... have nests, but the Son of

Man has nowhere to lay his head' (v.20). Our Lord went to great pains to make sure that people understood Him. But He went to great pains also to make sure that He was not misunderstood.

Frank and fearless

We have another example of our Lord's ability to get to grips with actualities and His refusal to allow His disciples to labour under any delusion.

As Jesus talks about going to Jerusalem and suffering many things at the hands of the elders, chief priests and teachers of the law, Peter remonstrates with Him and tries to steer Him away from the subject. Peter and the other disciples – let's face it – were somewhat taken up with dreams of imperial power despite our Lord's oft-repeated declaration of the true character of His kingdom. Does our Lord, in the interests of expediency, allow the minds of His disciples to be dominated by such dreams? He does not. He turns to Peter and says, 'Get behind me, Satan! You are a stumbling-block to me; you do not have in mind the things of God, but the things of men' (Matt. 16:23). Strong words.

One commentator suggests that the phrase 'Jesus turned' indicates that *Jesus turned pale* at the thought of one of His disciples trying to deter Him from the very purpose for which He had come to earth. Somewhat fanciful perhaps, but there can be little doubt that Peter's remonstration had a great effect on our Lord and evoked from Him an extraordinary response. Jesus was a completely frank and fearless Person. Therefore, because He said 'If it were not so, I would have told you' in connection with the existence of heaven, we can be sure that He meant what He said and that we can take Him at His Word. 'I would have told you.' He would indeed.

> Jesus was a completely frank and fearless Person.

We can trust those words to be true. And why? Because we can see that in His relationship with His followers He was always frank and fearless. He would never hide the truth from them to spare their feelings. Yet another example of this is the story in Mark 10:17–31.

A very rich young man runs up to Jesus, falls at His feet and asks, 'What must I do to inherit eternal life?' Our Lord's answer is clear and pointed: keep the commandments, do not murder, do not commit adultery, and so on. The young man claims that as far as keeping the commandments is concerned he is a rigid observer. However, Jesus looks into his soul and sees that even though on the surface he may pass the test of being a commandment-keeper there is entwined around his heart the love of riches.

Now note what it says in verse 21: 'Jesus looked at him and loved him.' But His love is not a sentimental type of love; it is a love that is strong enough to confront. With a characteristic thrust of His rapier-like logic, Jesus cuts right to the core issue and says, 'Go, sell everything you have and give to the poor' (v.21). The young man is nonplussed. His true god is his wealth and he is not prepared to give it up. Yet again our Lord demonstrates that His love is the kind that never hides the truth even though it may hurt a person's feelings. He is candid no less than kind.

No concealment

It would be easy to go through the Gospels multiplying examples to prove the realism and candour of Christ, but I think the three examples we have looked at are enough. When we deal with Jesus we deal with One who will never allow us to be misled, labour under a delusion or put our faith in a falsehood.

But just in case I have painted a one-sided picture of Jesus by showing Him to be a tough realist, let me introduce you to the thought that He is not just the Christ of candour but also the Christ of compassion. To put it another way: He is not just tough but tender. And the tenderness of His heart would not have allowed Him, while in possession of the facts, to conceal them from His followers. He knew full well how men and women longed for some sure word concerning the curtained future; He knew that the question of what lies beyond the grave was something that weighed heavily on their souls; He understood the concern and feelings of their hearts when they contemplated death.

How could Christ, with such a heart of compassion, have remained silent when He was the only One in the world who could pierce the veil and enlighten people on what lay beyond? How could He withhold the truth when to utter it would bring such solace to troubled souls? He, being who He was, simply had to speak out, to say, 'If it were not so, I would have told you.' Not to have done so would have been unthinkable.

Can you imagine Columbus after having discovered America wanting to keep the matter to himself? Or Captain Cook after exploring New Zealand wishing to leave the world ignorant of his findings? Both of these situations are unthinkable given the character and ideals of the men concerned. Likewise, it is unthinkable that Jesus, having spent eternity past in the presence of His Father, would not want to tell His followers something of the glories of that wondrous world. He says in effect, 'If seventy years of life, more or less, is all you could expect, I would be frank with you and urge you to make the most of it, but in My Father's house ...'

It is said that Professor T.H. Huxley, the famous agnostic (who, by the way, invented the term 'agnostic' and applied it to himself), reversed his views prior to his death and came to believe in God and a future life. As he lay dying (so his nurse reported) he raised himself on his elbows and gazed into the distance as if surveying some invisible scene, then dropped back on his pillow and murmured, 'So it was true! So it was true!'

We, who follow Christ, need no such revelation to convince us of the reality of heaven. It is enough that we have heard Him say, 'In my Father's house are many rooms; if it were not so, I would have told you' (John 14:2). He needs no vision who has heard that word.

Further Study

Luke 10:1–18; John 1:1–18

1. What did Jesus declare He had witnessed?
2. What did John declare about the pre-existent Christ?

Matt. 5:13–18; 18:3–4; 18:13

3. What did Jesus often link to the phrase 'I tell you the truth'?
4. What else did He link to heaven?

John 6:25–38; 3:31; 8:23; 13:3

5. What did Jesus say of His origin?
6. What did Jesus know?

CHAPTER FOUR

KEEPING HEAVEN IN VIEW

Hebrews 11:1–10;
2 Corinthians 4:5–18;
Philippians 1:12–26

*'So we fix our eyes on not on what is seen, but
on what is unseen. For what is seen is temporary,
but what is unseen is eternal.'*
2 Corinthians 4:18

We move on now to consider the suggestion that heaven should never be far from our minds as we make our way through this world. Some might respond to this by saying: Surely the constant consideration of heaven will interfere with work we have to do here on earth. Well, of course it can, but what I am talking about is a balanced view of the matter – not too little and not too much.

My reading of Christian history has brought me to the conclusion that the Christians who did most for this world in which we live were those who thought a good deal about the next. It could be argued, and argued successfully I think, that Christians who never allow themselves to think of the world that lies beyond are largely ineffective in this. If the truth be known, most of us go through life with our eyes cast downwards. We neither look nor long for heaven. Those whose eyes are never lifted up to see what lies ahead should not be surprised if they find the things of earth becoming more important to them than heaven, time becoming more important than eternity.

The constant remembrance that we are bound for 'a city whose architect and builder is God' will help us keep matters in perspective. It will enable us to hold onto things loosely, knowing that they are merely temporal. I think it was Cardinal Newman who said, 'Only those work with full effectiveness for the new Jerusalem below who see the New Jerusalem above. They make it after "the pattern which has been shown to them on the mount".

Between two gardens

Why is it that, generally speaking, we do not walk through this world with the prospect of heaven central to our thinking? One reason could be that we reckon we can have heaven now. A large percentage of believers appear to hold the view that being a Christian means we will no longer have to wrestle with problems or struggle with our finances and that we will never get sick.

Now let me say right away that I have seen too many miracles not to believe in them, and I am convinced that many of us are slow to avail ourselves of the resources of the abundant life found in Jesus Christ. God is willing to bless His people; indeed He delights in it. It is not wrong to ask God to resolve a difficult problem, to heal a serious sickness, or even work a miracle to help you when in financial difficulty. I have seen Him work in my own life in all of the ways I have just mentioned, and expect to see Him do the same in the future. That said, however, our view of the Christian life will be an unbalanced one if we think that life in Christ means that we never have to face problems or struggle with difficulties.

When Adam and Eve were expelled from the Garden of Eden, God put a 'Celestial Bouncer' at the entrance to stop them getting back in. Now we live outside the garden in a world that is cursed because of sin. Another garden awaits us, but that lies up ahead. Meanwhile we must live in a garden that, though still quite beautiful, has thorns and weeds. Those who ignore this fact have a very unbalanced view of Christianity.

We were designed for a world different to the one in which we are presently living. God never intended for us to struggle with sickness, wrestle with guilt, undergo deep bouts of melancholy and gloom or face the awful fact of death.

It is true that because of what Christ did for us on the cross, which was endorsed by the resurrection and the ascension, we have forgiveness for our sins (a sure remedy for guilt) and the promise of the Holy Spirit's help and comfort as we make our way through this world. But the world we inhabit is still fallen for all that – it is a world for which we were not designed. This is why even when we are joyful the joy we experience is a 'marred joy'. By that I mean that even in our happiest moments we will experience a degree of sadness that arises from the fact we are in an unnatural environment – unnatural in the sense that a departure from God's intentions is unnatural.

> Another garden awaits us, but that lies up ahead.

We must get to grips with this fact or else we will become disillusioned and disappointed. Oswald

Chambers was right when he said, 'Life is more tragic than orderly.' This is a tough world – a world still reeling from the effects of the Fall. Not to recognise or understand this means our expectations will be higher than they should be and our disappointments deeper than they need be.

Think with me for a moment before we continue discussing some of the points we have made. The prospect of heaven is something we should always keep before us. It helps us gain a right perspective on everything. Some believe we can have heaven now: 'Health and wealth until the day we die.' This is nonsense, of course, and quite unscriptural. Yes, God does answer prayer in the way we desire and does work miracles – but not always. Sometimes He lets His people suffer. And it is no good saying the ones who suffer have no faith. That is a cop-out. And a cruel cop-out. The Church needs a theology of suffering to balance its theology of miracles.

We live in a world for which we were not designed – hence we experience a marred joy. At our best moments we are aware that what we are experiencing is not the fullness of what we were made for. This is not negative thinking; it is realism. And facing the reality does not diminish the joy; rather, it helps prevent us pretending that what we have is better than it is. This is Christian realism – a factor missing in many sections of today's Church.

Consider the apostle's statement in 2 Corinthians

4:5–18. Clearly he was struggling but he was struggling well. Though he was crushed and perplexed (I wonder what about?) he kept his eyes on the unseen (v.18). He knew there was a better world to come, and the prospect of that helped to nerve him forward. It always does. The critics of Christianity call this escapism. But you could never call Paul an escapist. He faced the reality of heaven that he might better face the realities of earth.

Think with me about this: after Christ had ascended to heaven the disciples might well have wondered how they could continue the work He had vouchsafed to them now that He was no longer with them. They had been a vacillating bunch even during the time He had been amongst them. How would they fare now that He was in heaven?

To their credit they obeyed the Lord's command to wait in Jerusalem until they were endued with divine power (Acts 1:8), and when He, the Holy Spirit came, the results were astonishing. The men who just a few weeks previously had deserted their Lord were filled with a new courage. The rabbits became ferrets. And from that day forward the staggering thing is this – not once do we read of the disciples crying out, 'If only the Master was with us now.' In some of the situations in which they found themselves it would have been natural for them to have expressed that wish – but on no occasion did it happen. They lived and acted as if the Master was there with them, right at their side.

Was it merely an illusion? No, for He was right there with them. Not physically of course. His body was in heaven but the Holy Spirit made His presence universal. It is a mystery of course, but what a blessed mystery.

Further Study

Col. 1:1–8; Titus 2:1–14; Heb. 6:19

1. How did Paul link time and eternity?
2. What does the hope of heaven give us?

Rom. 8:18–27; 15:4; Heb. 6:18

3. What does Paul say about the whole of creation?
4. What does he set against this?

Heb. 11:31–40; Psa. 42:1–11

5. What were some of the experiences of these men and women of faith?
6. How did the psalmist talk to himself on such occasions?

CHAPTER FIVE

DESIGNED FOR BETTER THINGS

Romans 8:18–39;
2 Corinthians 5:1–10;
Philippians 1:12–26

'… *but we ourselves, who have the firstfruits of the*
Spirit, groan inwardly as we wait eagerly for our
adoption as sons, the redemption of our bodies.'
Romans 8:23

Even the most casual observer of the Christian life ought to be convinced that we were not made for the kind of world in which we live. We were designed for better things. However, because sin has entered this fair creation, we live now in a fallen world. And until that better world comes along we yearn for what we do not have.

The apostle Paul tells us that the whole creation groans (Romans 8:18–27). Everything that lives is subject to disease, death and decay. Some sensitive Christians say that when they are at prayer they can sometimes hear the 'groan' that is in creation. One described it to me as 'like an imprisoned energy desperately trying to escape'.

Have you sung the hymn 'All things bright and beautiful' recently? It is a lovely hymn but the woman who wrote it was not looking at the whole of creation, just some of it. She talks in one verse about 'The cold wind in the winter' it is true, but no verse concentrates on those parts of creation which are not pleasant to contemplate – animals that tear each other apart, for example. She was being selective for the purpose of the hymn. That is not meant to be a criticism. However, Paul, when he looked at creation, looked at it as a whole. Some of creation is 'bright and beautiful', but sin has made other parts of it downright ugly.

Groaning within ourselves

But not only does creation groan; we do also. 'We ourselves,' says the apostle Paul, 'groan inwardly' as we wait for sin and its effects to be banished from the universe (Rom. 8:23). Note it is we who are indwelt by the Spirit who groan in this way. Unbelievers don't share this experience. The Holy Spirit sensitises our souls to the fact that down here there is something wrong with almost everything. We must not allow this to fill us with gloom but we must accept it nevertheless.

Some Christians refuse to face this aspect of the Christian life and prefer instead to focus on other aspects of the Spirit's ministry, such as love, joy, peace, and so on. But to have peace and joy and yet groan inwardly is a tension with which Christians have to live. If all we had was joy and peace how strange it would be. We would make our way through life thinking only about ourselves and blissfully indifferent to the plight of the whole creation – animate and inanimate. It is this groan that keeps us balanced, knowing that perfection cannot be brought about by human methods.

Perfection cannot be brought about by human methods.

Elsewhere in Romans the apostle said that we are 'unspiritual, sold as a slave to sin' (Rom. 7:14). Is it any wonder when we think of the evil that sin has done in the world (and still continues to do) that we groan within ourselves? Do not deny this groan which is an inevitable result of the Spirit's indwelling. I would not dare to twist Scripture by writing 'The heritage of the Spirit is ... a groan.' But it is not far from the truth, is it?

Some may find it difficult to follow Paul's reasoning when he speaks of a groan being a Christian's heritage. We much prefer the idea of feeling the Spirit's joy, but as we have been seeing, groaning is part of our experience also. You may wish that Paul had given us further teaching on this subject, or at least made things somewhat clearer. If that is your reaction then I am sure you will not be offended when I say that you must take the matter up with him. One preacher I heard said when dealing with a difficult passage of Paul's: 'It is my business to expound him, not improve him.'

Consider with me a little more about this matter of living with the tension of joy on the one hand and a groan on the other. Those who sense only the joy of the Christian life and know nothing of the groan live life on a very insensitive level. They go on from day to day thinking only of themselves and are half-deaf to the cries of suffering humanity. They never give a thought to the fact that a large section of the world's population is hungry, and many are even starving. To be blind to this fact (and there are many others) means we will be unable to demonstrate Christ's compassion. Those who sense only the groan and never enter into the joy that the Spirit gives can, conversely, quickly become over-whelmed by the problems of the world and their spirits cast down with melancholy and gloom.

Living with this tension is not easy, but we are called to do so nevertheless. Clearly Paul lived with it. So must we.

Doing what the Father does

Life on this sin-cursed planet is a struggle and sometimes a strain. There are some, I know, who will say, 'Come on now, let's not be too pessimistic. Life can be bad but it can also be a ball.'

During a talk I gave to a group of ministers and leaders in Borneo some time ago I mentioned the quotation from Oswald Chambers: 'Life is more tragic than orderly.' Afterwards a man came up to me and commented, 'In my opinion, if we looked at the world through more optimistic eyes we would see that everything is beautiful.'

'I am glad you think so,' I said, 'but don't be too hard on me if I take a more sombre view of things.' Prior to giving the address I had spoken to a young woman in her early twenties who told me that she felt called to serve the Lord and was about to enter Bible college. However, her doctor had informed her that she was suffering from a terminal illness. She asked me to pray that God would heal her – and I did. But I was also aware that the surgery she was scheduled to undergo might not be successful and that there might not be a direct healing from God either. I would love to hear that she has been healed – God does heal people of terminal illnesses – but the reality is that sometimes He does not.

How then should we approach such situations? We should ask our Father in heaven what to pray for and how to pray. In John 5:1–23 we see Jesus healing just one out of a whole group of needy people. Why only one? In verse 19 we are told He looked first to heaven to see what His Father was doing and then He joined hands in ministering towards that self-same end.

Comfort from the promise

Throughout the Church's history God's people when faced by life's problems have drawn comfort from the promise of heaven. How, for instance, did slaves in America endure their afflictions? The 'Negro Spirituals', as they are called, give us the clue. They sang often of the prospect of heaven. The promise that one day we will be with Jesus in a perfect world has a powerful effect on our lives in the present and enables us to cope with difficult situations because it gives us that most precious of all ingredients – hope. It is like a doctor saying to a woman in labour, 'Hold on, the baby you long for will soon be in your arms. Now you feel pain but soon you will feel pleasure.' Awaiting us in heaven is a happiness that is beyond description.

Paul tells us that he longed to get to heaven but because his presence was more necessary on earth he was willing to stay (Phil. 1:23–24). One preacher I heard remarked, 'Paul was eager to go but willing to stay. We are willing to go but eager to stay.' Have you noticed how often Paul used the prospect of heaven to help him overcome the trials of this life? Think, for example, of these words: 'I consider that our present sufferings are not worth comparing with the glory that will be revealed in us' (Rom. 8:18). A friend of mine says, 'Here on earth there is something wrong with everything. In heaven there will be nothing wrong with anything.' Here we sojourn; there we belong.

I maintain we will carry out all the work that concerns God's purposes on this earth with skill and thoroughness because by faith we have the perfect always in view.

Further Study

Rom.2:1–9; Matt. 24:1–13; John 16:33

1. How did Jesus describe the end of the world?
2. What did Jesus say we would experience in the world?

2 Cor. 5:1–10; John 15:19; 18:36

3. What are the two dimensions to our spiritual groan?
4. What was Paul's preference?

Acts 24:1–16; Prov. 14:32; Titus 2:11–15

5. What was Paul's testimony to Felix?
6. How should we live in the light of heaven?

CHAPTER SIX

INTO THE FATHER'S PRESENCE

Acts 7:48–60;
John 14:15–31;
Corinthians 15:35–58;
Psalm 23:1–6

*'Even though I walk through the valley of the shadow
of death, I will fear no evil, for you are with me ...'*
Psalm 23:4

No discussion on the subject of heaven can be complete unless we are prepared to take a look at the mode of our departure to the heavenly city. And what is that mode of departure? It is through death. That is the issue to which we turn our attention now.

When I was newly converted (in my teens) I used to think to myself: Wouldn't it be wonderful if, when the time came for us to leave this world, God would just whisk us away and put us down in heaven without the necessity of having to experience death. Alas, sin has affected human life to such a degree that our bodies have become corruptible and thus have to be left behind at the door of death. 'Flesh and blood cannot inherit the kingdom of God' (1 Cor.15:50). Death has been described as a toll bar. At a toll-bar or gate one has to pay 'dues'. The body in which you and I live is one of the 'dues' which has to be paid. It belongs to this earth. We live here in a material world, and the only way we can correspond with our environment is through a material form. But heaven is a spiritual plane and thus this 'form' must be left behind. Let it return to the earth from whence it came. It has served its purpose.

William James, the well-known psychologist and philosopher of a past era, was once asked, 'Do you believe in personal immortality?'

'Yes of course I do,' he retorted, 'and ever more strongly as I get older.'

'Why?' questioned the enquirer.

'Because,' he replied, 'I am just getting fit to live.' The life inside him was bursting at the seams. For that reason he had no qualms about having to pay his toll-bar 'dues'. They put him on the road to life – real life.

Fallen asleep

Our Lord Jesus Christ said very little about the conditions of life hereafter, but the fact of survival underlies all He uttered. We have already had cause to delight in His plain words: 'In my Father's house are many rooms; if it were not so, I would have told you' (John 14:2). How can a Christian view death as a terror when all it does is usher him or her into the Father's presence?

Notice also that in the story of Jairus' daughter in Mark 5:35–43 Christ used the term 'sleep' where others would have used the term 'death'. To the mourners standing around the breathless body of the little girl He said, 'The child is not dead but asleep.' Now some interpret the incident like this: the people around thought the girl was dead but actually she was only asleep; Jesus knew this and thus only needed to heal her and did not, as is commonly supposed, bring her back from death. What then do such interpreters make of our Lord's words in John 11:11 in which He refers to the death of Lazarus in this way: 'Our friend Lazarus has fallen asleep'? There can be absolutely no doubt that Lazarus was, by our definition, dead. Why did Jesus use the word 'sleep' when talking about death? Because He saw it in its true perspective – as falling asleep in one world to awaken in another.

Of course the world in which one awakens depends on one's relationship to Jesus Christ. Those who do not know Christ and have not had their sins forgiven and received the assurance of eternal life will see death as far more sinister than just falling asleep. And rightly so. Nothing can be more disastrous than to fall asleep in this world and wake up in a world where Christ is not.

> Falling asleep in one world to awaken in another.

Vita! Vita! Vita!

The early Christians, we are told, carved on the walls of their prisons the words 'Vita! Vita! Vita!' which means 'Life! Life! Life!' Prison walls could not stifle the life that was in them because it was *eternal* life. Eternal life is a life that death cannot extinguish. By its very nature it is bound to extend beyond the limits of this life. Can the shell confine the growing seed? Of course not, and neither can earth's circumstances quench the life of God that is in the soul of the man or woman who has entered into a personal relationship with Jesus Christ.

Have you noticed that Jesus never used the word 'immortality' when speaking of the future life? He preferred the phrase 'eternal life' because that conveyed not merely duration but a quality of life so rich, so abundant, so inexhaustible, that it could not be confined to this present existence. 'Eternal life,' said one preacher, 'is a quality of life as different from the ordinary life as the ordinary life is different from the animal life.'

When Charles Kingsley, the novelist, was approaching death he said, 'God forgive me if I am wrong, but I look forward to it with an immense and reverent curiosity.' And Thomas Carlyle said, 'Eternity, which cannot be far off now, is my one strong city. I look into it fixedly now and then. All terrors about it seem superfluous.' How different from the words I once heard an agnostic utter at his brother's grave: 'Goodbye my brother ... this is the end of all things.' A Christian says of death: 'This is not the end; this is the beginning.'

'Hope beyond the grave'

A funeral director once told me he had observed that Christians handle death in a much better way than those who are not Christians. I asked him why he thought that was. After pausing for a few moments he said, 'I suppose it's because Christians have a hope beyond the grave.' Simple, but profound. The word 'hope' is a word that has to be clarified, however, for it has come to mean different things to different people. Some think of hope as a poor precarious thing, an illusion, a vanity. But hope is not so thought of in the New Testament. Paul makes hope one of the cardinal virtues of the Christian life.

How does this sharp contrast arise between those who regard hope as an illusion and those who regard it as a cardinal virtue? The answer is not difficult. Each group is talking about something different. There is a higher and lower hope. There is the real thing and the counterfeit; there is gold and there is gilt. What the world often describes as hope is really nothing more than optimism. Optimism, of course, is better than pessimism. The pessimist says, 'I suppose there is no milk in that jug.' The optimist says, 'Pass the milk please.'

The hope the Bible talks about, however – the hope of life beyond the grave – is more than optimism. It is based on an incontrovertible fact – the resurrection of Jesus from the dead. Jesus not only proclaimed life after death; He demonstrated it. Without that demonstration belief in immortality would not have much going for it. Now it has everything going for it. Everything!

Do you remember the story concerning the painting by G.F. Watts entitled 'Hope'? The picture shows a blind-folded woman sitting with bowed head on a sphere and holding in her hand a lyre. All the strings of the lyre are broken except one, and only one star shines in the dark-ened sky. Those who do not understand symbols find the meaning difficult to grasp. Two tramps who had crept into the gallery to escape from the cold looked up at it and one said, ' "Hope"? Why is it called "Hope"?' The other, gazing at the figure perched precariously on the sphere, replied, 'I suppose because she hopes she won't fall off.'

That is how many interpret hope. They see it, as I said yesterday, as a poor precarious thing. But the hope we Christians have for a better life beyond death is based, we concluded, on the resurrection of Christ. Jesus not only proclaimed life after death – He demonstrated life after death.

Jesus demonstrated life after death.

Some critics have claimed that the disciples stole Jesus' body while the soldiers who were on guard slept. Do the disciples come across in the book of Acts as men who harboured a guilty secret? Do they look like body-snatchers? No, they ploughed their way through persecution, sang their way through prisons and danced their way through death. For what? A hoax? Well hoaxes do not produce hallelujahs nor does body-snatching transform lives. Like produces like.

Because He lives

Perhaps the most significant reason why Christians do not fear death in the same way that non-Christians fear it is because we know for a fact that Jesus is alive, and because He lives we also will live, as John 14:19 powerfully puts it.

Two irreligious men were discussing the resurrection, telling each other why they found it impossible to accept it. Just then an old man whom they knew to be a Christian walked by. Stopping him they enquired, 'Sir, tell us why you believe that Jesus Christ rose from the dead.'

'Well,' said the old man, 'one reason is that I was talking to Him only a few minutes ago.'

Those who have surrendered themselves to Jesus Christ know Him to be alive because He lives within them. The historical has become the experimental. The fact of a living Christ is the best corroborated fact in history.

Some will disagree with that statement I am sure, but not those who know Christ as their Lord and Saviour. In every generation, and every geographical location, men and women who have received Christ experience the same thing – the knowledge that Christ is alive, redeeming, radiant, joy-producing, love-creating and heaven-assuring. We who are His do not merely remember Him; we realise Him. Heaven for us is a certainty because we experience something of it now. The hereafter is what we are after because we have tasted it down here. A daughter asked her Scottish father if he needed the Bible read to him as he lay dying. 'Na, lassie,' he said, 'I thatched my house before the storm began.'

Death's mission

Whether or not we are Christians, there is something in us all that shrinks from what we regard as the grim angel of death. Many Christians have said to me, 'I am not afraid to die but I am anxious about the way in which I will die. Will I be in pain? Will I linger long? Will I be a burden to my loved ones?' All these are legitimate questions and should not be ignored. Whatever the circumstances of our dying, we must never forget that Christ will be with us to the end. But what we must remember above all is this: death has but one mission, and that is to conduct us into the presence of our Heavenly Father and to give us a permanent place in the great company of the redeemed.

A preacher friend of mine tells how he became lost in the centre of a large city when he was a little boy. As soon as he realised he was lost he dissolved into floods of tears and a kindly policeman took him by the hand and led him to the police station. There he waited for a couple of hours in a rather dismal room until his father was traced and summoned to come and fetch him. When a stern officer (at least, that is how the officer appeared to him) came to reunite him with his father he cried harder than ever because he did not quite know where he was being taken or why. But in a room at the far end of a dark corridor he saw his father and suddenly his tears dried up. He clung to him and laughed at the folly of being afraid when the stern policeman was simply leading him to his father.

It will not be much different when we die. Jesus spoke of 'my Father's house' (John 14:2). In childlike anticipation of the Father's house let's work until the day is done.

Further Study

1 Cor. 15:1–58; 1 Thess. 4:13–14; Matt. 5:4

1. What is distinctive about Christian grief?
2. Why does Paul say we can stand firm?

2 Cor. 5:1–10; 1 John 3:1–3; 1 Cor. 13:12

3. How does Paul put it?
4. What does John declare that we know?

John 3:12–21; 5:24; 12:25; Gal. 6:8

5. How did Jesus define eternal life?
6. What is the difference between eternal and everlasting?

CHAPTER SEVEN

CHOOSING THE RIGHT ROAD

Matthew 7:1–13;
John 10:1–18;
Ephesians 2:11–22;
2 Peter 3:1–18;
Revelation 22:12–21

*'Enter through the narrow gate. For wide is the
gate and broad the road that leads to destruction,
and many enter through it.'*
Matthew 7:13

No consideration of heaven would be complete without reflecting on its opposite – hell. This is what we turn to now. Hell is not a pleasant subject to discuss but we must reflect upon it nevertheless. The doctrine of hell is something that modern-day Christians are either reluctant to speak about or are throwing overboard. But whatever we think of the issue, belief in hell has the full support of Scripture. Moreover, hell is a subject about which our Lord spoke often.

Two centuries ago, William Blake wrote a book entitled *The Marriage of Heaven and Hell* in which he attempted to argue that reality never presents us with an 'either-or' and that, given time, evil will be turned into good without the necessity of a final and total rejection. This is an increasingly popular viewpoint, and one that is being endorsed by many liberal theological colleges nowadays.

In response to *The Marriage of Heaven and Hell* C.S. Lewis wrote his little volume entitled *The Great Divorce*. In it he pointed out that we are not living in a world where the roads are the radii of a circle that, if followed long enough, will lead to the centre. Instead (as our Lord told us in Matthew 6:13–14), the roads lead in different directions – to heaven or to hell. But being on the wrong road – the broad road – does not inevitably mean that one will finish up in hell. One can choose to turn off it and take the other road – the narrow road – that leads to life and to heaven.

God's great rescue plan

The great rescue plan which our Lord Jesus Christ initiated when He came to this earth enables us to move from one road to the other.

The idea that eventually all evil will be refined to such a degree that there will be a marriage between heaven and hell is preposterous and holding it is a terrible error. As C.S. Lewis put it: 'Good, as it ripens, becomes continually more different not only from evil but from other good. A wrong sum can be put right, but only by going back till you find the error and working it afresh from that point, never by simply going on.' Those who believe that hell can be refined so that it is eventually wedded to heaven sometimes base their reasoning on Paul's words in Romans 8:28 where he speaks about all things being worked together for good. But Paul was not referring there to hell; he was talking about life here on this planet. What is more, he made it clear that the transmutation of bad into good takes place only in the lives of those 'who love him, who have been called according to his purpose'.

Our Lord's great rescue plan accomplished for us on the cross is the only answer to hell. Because of this no one goes to hell just because they are bad and no one goes to heaven just because they are good. They go to either one of those two places according to their relationship with Jesus Christ.

Either–or

Let us be clear about one matter – there are only two places of final destination. One is called heaven, the other is called hell. In Matthew 5:21–30 our Lord presents us with a most solemn challenge. He makes it clear that in this matter of hell it is 'either–or'. Either we give up our sinful way of life or we face a future in hell.

> There are only two places of final destination.

These are stark and shocking words but it would be foolish to ignore them. If we insist on holding on to our sinful ways then we shall not see heaven. If we want to reach heaven then we must make up our minds that some things must go. Evil things I mean. The eye looks at things which we approach, then may grasp and possess. So we must watch what we see, for seeing creates desire and desire creates emotion, and in the battle between the will and the emotion the emotion almost always wins. The hand is the part of us that takes hold, that grasps what we want. Never take hold of something without realising that the thing you grasp may very well take hold of you.

What Jesus is saying in this passage, you see, is this: we must have a disciplined spirit that rejects those things that heaven rejects. We must be firm with ourselves if we are serious about heaven for, as I said before, our hereafter is determined by what we are after here. I think I can say with certainty that those who get to heaven will not regret for one moment what they abandoned here on earth, no matter how drastic the severance may have been. For the compensations will be beyond all telling.

Surrendering the will

One of the saddest things that is happening in our day (in Christian circles I mean) is the movement away from the traditional belief in an everlasting hell. More liberally-minded Christians are embracing 'universalism' – the belief that everyone will ultimately be saved and reach heaven. In contrast, many evangelical Christians are embracing the theory known as 'annihilationism' – the belief that only Christians will live for ever because sinners will be totally annihilated.

There may be some arguments for annihilationism (though I am not convinced by them myself), but there is no argument whatsoever for universalism – the assumption that everyone will finish up in heaven. The theory does not take into consideration the tremendous power of the human will. When God gave us a will He did so knowing full well that we could use its power not only for Him but against Him. Nevertheless He chose to bestow upon us this awesome power. Our joy as individuals lies in the surrender of that will to the Creator, but it has to be a surrender. God will not force us to do anything.

I would love with all my heart to be able to build my writing ministry around the idea that all will be saved.

However, I have to agree with C.S. Lewis who put the whole issue into a true perspective when he said: 'When people say all will be saved my reason retorts: "Without their will or with it?" If I say "Without their will" I at once perceive a contradiction. How can the supreme voluntary act of self-surrender be involuntary? If I say "With their will" my reason replies "How if they *will not* give in?" '

But what if a person will not surrender? What is the destiny of such an individual?

Let me tell you about a certain man I once knew, a man I consider to be the most contemptible person I have ever met. Though he was a fairly wealthy man he treated his wife (a member of a church I pastored) as if she was a piece of dirt. He bullied his children, used the most foul language to everyone, and laughed uproariously at the idea of God. 'If God exists,' I heard him say, 'then He is no different than I am. He doesn't seem to care two figs for the universe ... and neither do I.' He died, as far as I can tell, impenitent. Just hours before his death he was heard to say, 'If there is a hell then that's where I want to be. I could never stand being with goody-goodies.'

Now we must be careful that we don't say to ourselves 'A man like that deserves hell' for that is not a Christian attitude. To want someone's eternal damnation is a sin. But suppose a man or woman will not bow their knees to Christ. What destiny is appropriate for them? To put them in heaven with the forgiven and the redeemed? To let them remain there for all eternity gloating over the fact that they have had the last laugh? Such an idea is untenable. The only appropriate destiny for those who stubbornly refuse to come to Christ is hell. To put them in heaven might be a worse hell than the one we are talking about. I say that not with any sense of gloating but out of a sense of being true to the facts.

Objections

What are the objections that people raise towards the idea of hell? There are many. This is not the place to consider them all but I want to focus on the one that is probably the most popular and most oft-repeated: *hell is incompatible with who God is*. You may have heard different forms of this argument. Sometimes it is presented like this: God is too good to send people to hell. Or: the Almighty is a forgiving Father so is it not reasonable to suppose that ultimately all will be forgiven?

Take the first version of the argument: God is too good to send people to hell. In actual fact God doesn't send anyone to hell. They go there of their own accord by refusing the offer of mercy and forgiveness that is found in Jesus Christ. Now take the second version: that *a loving Heavenly Father will ultimately forgive everyone*. This objection is based on a misconception of forgiveness. Forgiveness is different from condonation.

When you condone something you decide to overlook it, to excuse it. Forgiveness has to be accepted in order for it to be complete, otherwise it is merely theoretical. A person who does not admit to any guilt will not be able to accept forgiveness. To quote C.S. Lewis again: 'The damned are, in one sense, successful rebels to the end; that the doors of hell are locked on the inside. I do not mean that the ghosts may not wish to come out of hell ... but they certainly do not will it. They enjoy for ever the horrible freedom they have demanded, and are therefore self-enslaved.'

> Forgiveness has to be accepted in order for it to be complete.

Wall of hostility

The final answer to all those who object to the doctrine of hell is this: God has done everything He can to rescue people from hell and the only ones to go there are those who choose to go there. It is no good mumbling that God should forgive their sins and give them a fresh start. He has already provided for that at Calvary. And how can God forgive those who do not wish to be forgiven?

If our perception of human nature was the same as God's I think we would discover something that would horrify us. I think we would see what the theologian Henri Nouwen describes as 'a clenched fist'. Ephesians 2:14 tells us that forming a barrier between us and God was a wall of hostility. The dictionary defines the word 'hostility' as a state of enmity or warfare. The nature with which we are born is not just disinterested in God; it hates Him. And it is there even in the 'nicest' of us – a basic attitude that shakes a clenched fist in the face of God. Some, no matter what, will never yield to the Creator. They prefer enmity to surrender; war to peace. What can be done with such people? Shouldn't they be left alone?

Well, alas, that is what hell is. The writer Dorothy Sayers once said, 'Hell is the enjoyment of one's own way for ever.' C.S. Lewis put it even more powerfully when he said that there are two classes of people in the universe: 'Those who say to God, "Thy will be done" – the saints. And those to whom God says, "Thy will be done" – the sinners.' In which class, I wonder, are you?

Further Study
Matt. 22:1–14; 8:5–12; 25:46
1. What did Jesus teach in this parable?
2. How did Jesus describe hell?

John 11:25; Heb. 10:19–22; 1 Tim. 2:5
3. What did Jesus declare to Martha?
4. What does the word 'mediator' mean?

Josh. 24:11–15; Deut. 30:19; 1 Kings 18:21
5. What proposition did Joshua put to the people?
6. What was his own response?

CHAPTER EIGHT

CITIZENS OF HEAVEN

John 1:1–18;
2 Corinthians 5:11–21;
Philippians 3:12–21;
1 Peter 3:8–22

'But our citizenship is in heaven.'
Philippians 3:20

We move on now to focus on an intriguing aspect of our theme: the fact, as Paul reminds us, that we are citizens of heaven (Phil. 3:20). What does being a citizen of heaven involve? Examine the context of this verse with me for a moment.

The apostle has just been talking about those whose minds are set on earthly things, those whom he describes as 'enemies of the cross of Christ' (v.18). True Christians, he is saying, look to the things that are eternal and set their minds on what is above. Philippi had the distinction of being a Roman colony, with all the privileges which that brought in the ancient world. But Paul wanted his Philippian readers to understand that they had a higher allegiance – they were citizens of heaven. To be a citizen of heaven means that though during our life here on the earth we obey the laws of the state, pay our taxes and act honourably and honestly in every circumstance, our supreme loyalty and love lie elsewhere. It is heaven's commands that prevail in our lives, and it is the mind of the King in heaven that we seek to know most of all.

The alien world in which we live influences us all. Its judgments affect us, its atmosphere is not conducive to our spiritual development, and its pressures bear on us in ten thousand ways. How easy it is, without us realising it, to become 'conformed to the world', as Paul warns us in Romans 12:2. We should be loyal subjects of the country in which we live, but that allegiance is secondary – first and foremost we are citizens of heaven.

Ambassadors of heaven

Each citizen is also required to be an ambassador, as Paul tells us: 'We are therefore Christ's ambassadors ...' (2 Cor. 5:20). Ambassadors! Personal representatives of our Heavenly King. Now, an ambassador's allegiance is to his own land and head of state. For instance, the American ambassador to Britain resides in London but his citizenship and love and loyalty belong to his home country.

First and foremost we are citizens of heaven.

It is a high privilege to be an ambassador. But there are also dangers associated with the role. According to Lord Templewood in his book *Ambassador on a Special Mission*, one of the dangers an ambassador faces is staying too long in the country to which he has been sent; that is to say, if he does not make frequent visits to his own land, breathe his own native air, reacquaint himself with his native customs and familiarise himself with all that is going on, he can quickly become 'denationalised'. He must return home frequently, absorb his own atmosphere, renew his strength by contact with his native soil so that he does not lose his orientation.

How can we who are citizens of heaven save ourselves from being not so much 'denationalised' but 'despiritualised'? By what means can we guard against this possibility? We must breathe the atmosphere of heaven by talking frequently to God in prayer, meditating on the Scriptures, and setting our 'hearts on things above, where Christ is seated at the right hand of God' (Col. 3:1). We must breathe as often as we can heaven's pure atmosphere.

Secrets of success

Let us remind ourselves how an ambassador from another country can get into difficulties. When he arrives in the country to which he has been sent at first he views matters from the perspective of his own native land, but gradually and half-unconsciously he begins to think to himself: 'There are different ways of looking at things.' As he absorbs the atmosphere of a foreign land and hears different viewpoints, little by little his perception begins to be affected, and if he fails to maintain a close connection with the country to which he belongs he is in danger of becoming 'denationalised'.

A wise old man told me not long after I had been converted: 'The secret of success in the Christian life is to realise that now you have a new nationality. You are Welsh by natural birth but because you have been born again you are now a citizen of heaven. If ever heaven's rules conflict with earth's rules then remember, heaven's rules must take precedence. And remember too,' he added, 'that the secret of success is prayer. Guard your daily quiet time with God. Speak to Him, listen to Him, and count as dangerous anything that causes you to lose your links with heaven.'

Heaven's rules must take precedence.

Those words 'count as dangerous anything that causes you to lose your links with heaven' still register in my spiritual memory. There is no way that a Christian ambassador can retain his or her true citizenship in this alien world without regular (preferably daily) prayer and meditation on the Scriptures. You must return whenever you can to your own environment.

On more than one occasion the apostle Paul found it highly convenient to claim his Roman citizenship. The great apostle was arrested in Jerusalem (see Acts 21:27–36) after unintentionally disturbing the peace, but he proved to be one of the strangest prisoners the commander (the chief captain) had ever taken into custody.

First, Paul astonished him by addressing him in Greek. The commander, who assumed he was an Egyptian, exclaimed: 'So you know Greek do you?' (21:37, Phillips). After he had been given permission to speak to the crowd, Paul surprised him still further by silencing them when he started to address them in perfect Aramaic. And when, following Paul's speech, a riot broke out, and soldiers were about to flog him, Paul had a further surprise up his sleeve. He said to the centurion standing by, 'Is it legal for you to flog a Roman citizen?' The centurion then sent for the commander, who came at once and asked Paul: 'Are you a Roman citizen?'

'Yes I am,' replied Paul. To which the commander responded, 'I had to pay a big price for my citizenship.'

'But I was born a citizen,' retorted Paul (Acts 22:22–29).

Roman citizenship could be acquired in several ways: by birth to Roman parents, on retirement from the army, after having been freed from slavery by a Roman master, as a gift from a Roman general or by purchase. There is, however, only one way to acquire citizenship in heaven: you have to gain it by birth. Not birth from below, but birth from above.

No other way

Multitudes of people still cling to the idea that they can become citizens of heaven in some way other than by birth. But the idea is false. I say again: the only way one can become a citizen of heaven is by birth.

Permit me to identify some of the false ideas which men and women hold concerning this matter of heavenly citizenship. Some believe it is possible to attain it by rigorous moral effort. In other words, you earn it through good works. But as one famous preacher put it – and His use of metaphor is quite brilliant – you cannot work your passage to heaven. Men and women have tried to do so in every age but they have always failed. The Pharisees attempted to work their way to heaven in Jesus' day. John Wesley tried this method too until he came to see that the crucial word in connection with the Christian life is not *do*, but *done*. Gaining admittance to heaven is not something we have to do but something that has been done for us on the cross by our Lord Jesus Christ.

A man once said to me, 'I never pass up a chance to do someone a good turn. I feel it is always the right thing to do. If there is a heaven then I expect to get into it. It is where I belong.' All the good turns in the world will not entitle us to citizenship in heaven. It is commendable to want to serve God, but first there must be reconciliation to Him. You can become a citizen of a country by earning the right, by living and working there for a while, but that is not the way to become a citizen of heaven.

One other false impression that people have concerning citizenship in heaven is that it can be passed on to them from their Christian parents. It is wonderful to have Christian parents. I thank God that both my parents were Christians and that, like Timothy, from a child I knew the Holy Scriptures. Godly parents can do many things: they can dedicate or christen us, they can teach us the principles of the faith, they can expose us to the worship of the Church, but there is one thing they cannot do – they cannot secure for us a place in heaven.

Hophni and Phineas had a good father in Eli, but they

brought shame on the nation of Israel. Absalom, too, had a good father, but he broke his father's heart and after his rebellion died a traitor. I can't tell you the number of times I have heard people say they felt they were covered by their Christian parents' lives and that God would accept them into heaven on the grounds of their parents' good works. This is an illusion.

Another false idea that people cling to is that they will gain citizenship in heaven by giving to good causes and by their charitable works. Generosity is not the means of reaching heaven – Jesus is. When I was a little boy my father wrote in the flyleaf of one of my Bibles: 'Money is a universal provider for everything but happiness and a passport everywhere but to heaven.' Money can buy you many things down here on earth but it has no power to gain you a place in heaven.

Gates of pearl

If we cannot purchase heavenly citizenship, earn it, or have it passed on to us by our parents how do we become citizens of the heavenly kingdom? We are invited to consider heaven as a city with twelve gates (Rev. 21:21). Some think the writer is portraying heaven in allegorical terms, but whether he is or not, it is clear he is describing a picturesque and beautiful place.

Notice that every gate into the New Jerusalem is made of pearl. I have often remarked that a pearl is a product of pain. When an oyster is invaded by something –

perhaps a grain of sand – it secretes a liquid which hardens and then becomes a pearl. I think the reason why the gates of the New Jerusalem are made of pearl is to convey to us that the entrance into the eternal city is through the wounds of Christ on the cross, now healed of course but remaining for ever the one and only way into the divine presence.

Catch the symbolism of this: the only way into the city of God is through a gate made of pearl. In other words, those who enter the city do so trusting the work that Christ did for them on the cross. You can't scale those jasper walls. You must go in through a gate – a gate made of pearl. Accept in penitence the sacrifice made on your behalf by Christ on the cross and nothing will stop you claiming citizenship of the divine kingdom. Permit me now to ask you this question: If you are not a citizen of heaven do you want to become one? If so, pray this prayer with me now:

Heavenly Father, I surrender my life to You today
and accept the sufferings of Your Son on the cross
as a sufficient guarantee of my entrance into heaven.
I turn from my sin and cast all my hope on You.
In Jesus' name I pray. Amen.

Further Study

Luke 22:24–30; 1 Pet. 1:4; Rev. 21:27

1. What did Jesus portray to the disciples?
2. What is the register of heaven's citizens?

John 3:1–11; 1:13; Titus 3:5

3. Why did Nicodemus struggle?
4. What did Jesus underline as components of new birth?

1 Pet. 1:13–23; 1 John 5:1; 2 Cor. 5:17

5. What is the 'imperishable seed'?
6. How do we know we are born of God?

CHAPTER NINE

'I JUST COULDN'T FIND THE WORDS'

Revelation 2:12–17; 4:1 – 5:14; 7:1–17; 22:1–11;
1 Corinthians 13:1–13;
Hebrews 13:7–21

'The throne of God and of the Lamb will be in the city, and his servants will serve him. They will see his face …'
Revelation 22:3–4

It is time now to come to grips with the question: What is heaven like? Though it is not possible to buy a guide book or a map of the celestial city, the book of Revelation, perhaps more than any other book of the Bible, gives us some idea of what heaven is like.

Whenever I come to the book of Revelation I am reminded of the story I once heard of a little girl who was born blind. Her mother used to describe the beauty of the world to her but the little girl, having never been able to see, did not have any real idea of what was being described. When she was twelve years old an operation was performed on her eyes which resulted in her gaining sight. When, for the first time, she saw the beauty of creation she turned to her mother and exclaimed, 'Oh Mother, why didn't you tell me it was so beautiful?'

Her mother responded, 'I tried, my darling ... I tried. But I just couldn't find the words.'

That is how I feel as I read John's description of heaven. He tries to tell us what it is like, but eloquent and descriptive as he is, one has the feeling that language is being stretched to the utmost.

Heaven is a place of perpetual praise.

In Revelation chapter 4 John shows us that heaven is a place of perpetual praise. All eyes in heaven seem to be directed towards the throne and every creature is vocal in the worship of God and of the Lamb. One of the great delights of earth is when the soul is caught up in praise of God. But in heaven we shall not just be caught up in it; we shall be lost in it. Here our praise is just a rehearsal; there it will be a realisation.

The focus of heaven's worship

From the description John gives of heaven it seems obvious that the first thing that struck him about it is the extent to which the Deity is praised. In Revelation chapter 4 God the Creator is the One who is being adored. In the following chapter the Lamb becomes the object of worship.

I don't know if you have noticed this but it is clear to me that the praise described in chapter 5 greatly exceeds that of chapter 4 – at least in terms of volume. Both chapters reveal that the twenty-four elders are engaged in worship, as are the four living creatures, and that they express their adoration with obvious sincerity and power. But see what chapter 5 records in addition: 'Then I looked and heard the voice of many angels, numbering thousands upon thousands, and ten thousand times ten thousand. They encircled the throne and the living creatures and the elders. In a loud voice they sang: "Worthy is the Lamb, who was slain, to receive power and wealth and wisdom and strength ..." ' (vv.11–12). It seems that when it comes to the worship of the Lamb the eternal rafters ring with anthems that roll and reverberate like thunder.

What can this be saying to us? I think it is saying that the focus of heaven's worship is the Lamb. Does this make the Father and the Holy Spirit envious? Of course not. Although the Lamb is the centre of worship, there is adoration of God the Father and implicit worship of God the Holy Spirit also; they too are an integral part of our redemption. Here on earth the Lamb is the focus of worship, and the same is true in heaven. As an old hymn puts it: *The Lamb is all the glory ... in Immanuel's land.*

Endless creativity

Is our time in heaven to be entirely filled with praise? Not according to Scripture. Humourists have had much fun depicting heaven as an interminable church service where mortals grow wings and are given a permanent place in the eternal choir. Lloyd George, one-time British prime minister (and a Welshman!) used to say that when he was a boy the idea of heaven used to terrify him more than hell because he thought of it as a perpetual Sunday. To understand his horror one must remember that in his day Sunday was quiet and solemn, and children were often required to stay indoors after they had attended church and do nothing but read. He claimed that his concept of heaven resulted in him turning to atheism, although in later years he came at least to accept the idea of God and of heaven.

In contrast, we are told that in heaven the redeemed serve Him day and night (Rev. 7:15). So heaven is not just a place of praise; it is a place of endless service also. One of the sweet things we experience down here on earth is the knowledge that we are working with God. It will be no less sweet, I believe, in heaven. There is nothing stagnant or static about the bliss of heaven. We serve a God whose creative ability is endless. 'My Father is always at his work,' Jesus said (John 5:17). Some take that to refer to God's work in redemption and say that when that work is complete He will stop. Yet I cannot believe God will ever be unemployed or go into retirement. He will be engaged in creative and endless efforts and we, the Church, will be at His side, working with Him.

But doesn't work bring weariness? It does down here on earth but not in heaven. As F.M. Knollis put it in these lyrical lines:

In that blessed world above
Work will not bring weariness
For work itself is love.

Thomas Carlyle, the writer, pictured God as sitting on a throne in eternity 'doing nothing'. That is not the way I imagine Him. I see Him as a Worker who will involve His children in working with Him in the kind of work that is purposeful and satisfying.

How different from the words of Henry Ward Beecher, the famous American preacher, who while walking with his father Lyman Beecher in Greenwood

Cemetery, New York, remarked, 'I suppose one day they will bring me out here and leave me, but I won't stay here.'

'Where will you be?' asked his father.

'I don't know exactly,' he replied, 'but somewhere right in the thick of things, working for God.' And that too is where you and I will be – right in the thick of things.

> 'Right in the thick of things, working for God.'

Indescribable joy

As well as being a place of praise and service heaven is a place of indescribable joy. Some Christian writers and commentators believe this is the greatest thing about heaven. C.S. Lewis wrote in one of his books: 'Joy is the serious business of heaven.'

Think how often heaven and joy are linked together in the New Testament. Jesus said on one occasion, 'There is joy before the angels of God over one sinner who repents' (Luke 15:10, RSV). And when telling the parable of the Talents He promised that those who use their talents and multiply them will hear the Master say, 'Enter into the joy of your master' (Matt. 25:21, RSV).

But won't heaven be tinged with sadness for some when they realise that their loved ones are in hell? Won't the final loss of one soul dampen the delights of those who are saved? One person has expressed this view: 'I can accept no salvation which leaves even one creature in the dark outside.' Now that sounds very compassionate but it does not take into account all aspects of the situation. Consider what would be involved if God were to respond to this attitude. It would mean that the stubborn and recalcitrant would be allowed to blackmail the universe, and hell would have the power to influence heaven.

I don't know whether or not there will be sadness in the hearts of those who find that some of their loved ones are in hell, but what I do know is that every one of us will see matters with far more clarity than we do now and will have God's perspective on the situation. Seeing clearly we will feel correctly. That is where we have to leave it.

Gales of laughter

A word that is associated with joy is laughter. Frequently I have been asked: Will there be laughter in heaven? Personally, I have no doubt about it. The God who made Sarah to laugh, does He not laugh Himself? I believe that gales of laughter will echo from the redeemed, and we shall discover, I think, that however much we have laughed down here on earth it will be as nothing compared to the laughter of heaven.

Scripture hints that there is laughter and joy in the heart of God. Why only hints? If the Lord veils His glory lest it be too bright for mortal eyes then might He not also veil His joy? One of the things I have noticed when sitting at the death bed of a Christian (that of my own wife included) is that sometimes they talk of hearing laughter. 'Can you hear that?' they have asked. 'Can you hear people laughing?'

Some time ago I was told about a little boy brought up in a poor and quarrelsome family who could not remember ever having laughed. After dark he would make his way to a neighbouring family whom he knew to be happy and sit beneath their window just to hear them laugh. Then he would go back home, lie on his bed and wonder if one day he would be able to laugh too.

Possibly I am imagining this but sometimes, when in prayer and listening for the voice of God's Spirit, I think I hear the laughter of heaven. I can tell you this with confidence: none of us have ever laughed down here the way we will laugh in heaven.

Perfection

We look now at yet another characteristic of heaven: it is a place of absolute perfection. In the last two chapters of the book of Revelation the apostle John uses a succession of negatives to help us develop a picture of heaven. There will be no more death, he says, no more crying, no more sorrow, no more pain, no longer any curse, no more night, and so on.

These last two chapters of Revelation are described by some commentators as 'The Chapters of the No More's'. A preacher friend of mine once amused his congregation with an unintentional pun when, after reading out the list of negatives in Revelation 21 and 22, he said, 'What a wonderful picture John paints with his No's'! Isaac Watts, thinking of the perfection of heaven, wrote these lines:

> *Then we shall see His face*
> *And never, never sin.*
> *There from the rivers of His grace*
> *Drink endless pleasures in.*

The reason for heaven's perfection is that sin, which is the cause of all imperfection, has no place or part in that eternal realm. But is it likely that sin will again break out in heaven? It did once with Lucifer. Might not someone mar its beauty and harmony by a collision of their will with God's? Have no fear. Sin will not only be impossible but unthinkable. As unthinkable for us as it will be for the Saviour to whom we will be joined.

So, heaven has four characteristics. It is a place of perpetual praise, a place of endless service, a place of ineffable joy and a place of absolute perfection. These are not the only characteristics of heaven, of course, but they are enough to whet our appetite for the day when we will meet up with our Lord and sit with Him at the marriage supper of the Lamb.

The final thought I want to leave with you is one that arises from Revelation 2:17: the fact that in heaven every one of us will have a new name. As you know, names in the Bible are not so much designations as descriptions.

The name Jacob stood for supplanter; the name Jesus for Saviour.

I'm not a number

There are hundreds of examples in Scripture of names describing a person's character – or lack of it. What is more personal to us than our names? We are easily offended when people refer to us as numbers. 'I am not a number, I am person with a name,' we say. It seems, however, that the new name we will be given in heaven will be a secret between God and each one of us. 'I will give him ... a new name ... known only to him who receives it.'

> Every one of us will have a new name.

What can we take this secrecy to mean? That every one of us will relate to God in a way that is personal. No one need fear that being part of a community means we will lose our personal relationship with the Trinity. You will not be lost in the crowd. Your relationship with God will be as personal (if not more so) as it is here. You will be part of a great host but it will also be as if it were just you and Your Father in heaven.

Homeward bound

What is our conclusion as we come to the end of reflecting together on this thrilling theme of heaven? It must be this: the one thought above all others that should dominate our thinking as we make our way through this alien world is that we are going home.

Let me tell you this story. Many years ago, on the East Coast of the United States, two ships passed each other – one a large sailing ship, the other a small steamer. The small steamer was just a run-down vessel that visited the ports on the East Coast, dropping off supplies such as tea, coffee, mechanical equipment and so on. The great sailing ship with its white sails billowing in the wind was a tremendous sight and the men on the small steamer caught the scent of spices and perfumes as it passed by. As was the custom in those days the captain of the little steamer picked up his megaphone and hailed the great sailing ship in this way: 'I am the captain of the *Mary Anne* and I have been out of Miami 12 days carrying little bits and pieces to the different ports. And I am on my way to New England. Who are you?' In response, a strong voice boomed out from the megaphone on the other ship: 'I am the *Begun of Bengal*, 123 days out of Canton, having delivered perfumes and spices to many ports of the world, and now, homeward bound.'

As Christians we can make a similar claim. We are happily engaged in dropping off the perfume of heaven on our way through this world, but our greatest joy is this: we are homeward bound.

Further Study

Rev. 21:1–7; Isa. 25:1–8; 35:10; 51:11; 60:20; Rev. 7:17
1. What is Zion a picture of?
2. What will replace it?

Matt. 10:29–31; Heb. 12:23; Psa. 139:13–18
3. How did Jesus illustrate God's intimate knowledge of us?
4. How did the psalmist express it?

John 1:26–36; 1 Cor. 5:7; 1 Pet. 1:19; Rev. 7:9
5. What did John declare?
6. What is the scene around the throne?

NATIONAL DISTRIBUTORS

UK: (and countries not listed below)
CWR, Waverley Abbey House, Waverley Lane, Farnham, Surrey GU9 8EP.
Tel: (01252) 784700 Outside UK +44 (0)1252 784700

AUSTRALIA: CMC Australasia, PO Box 519, Belmont, Victoria 3216.
Tel: (03) 5241 3288

CANADA: Cook Communications Ministries, PO Box 98, 55 Woodslee
Avenue, Paris, Ontario.
Tel: 1800 263 2664

GHANA: Challenge Enterprises of Ghana, PO Box 5723, Accra.
Tel: (021) 222437/223249 Fax: (021) 226227

HONG KONG: Cross Communications Ltd, 1/F, 562A Nathan Road,
Kowloon.
Tel: 2780 1188 Fax: 2770 6229

INDIA: Crystal Communications, 10-3-18/4/1, East Marredpally,
Secunderabad – 500 026.
Tel/Fax: (040) 7732801

KENYA: Keswick Books and Gifts Ltd, PO Box 10242, Nairobi.
Tel: (02) 331692/226047 Fax: (02) 728557

MALAYSIA: Salvation Book Centre (M) Sdn Bhd, 23 Jalan SS 2/64,
47300 Petaling Jaya, Selangor.
Tel: (03) 78766411/78766797 Fax: (03) 78757066/78756360

NEW ZEALAND: CMC Australasia, PO Box 36015, Lower Hutt.
Tel: 0800 449 408 Fax: 0800 449 049

NIGERIA: FBFM, Helen Baugh House, 96 St Finbarr's College Road,
Akoka, Lagos.
Tel: (01) 7747429/4700218/825775/827264

PHILIPPINES: OMF Literature Inc, 776 Boni Avenue, Mandaluyong City.
Tel: (02) 531 2183 Fax: (02) 531 1960

REPUBLIC OF IRELAND: Scripture Union, 40 Talbot Street, Dublin 1.
Tel: (01) 8363764

SINGAPORE: Armour Publishing Pte Ltd, Block 203A Henderson Road, 11–06 Henderson Industrial Park, Singapore 159546.
Tel: 6 276 9976 Fax: 6 276 7564

SOUTH AFRICA: Struik Christian Books, 80 MacKenzie Street, PO Box 1144, Cape Town 8000.
Tel: (021) 462 4360 Fax: (021) 461 3612

SRI LANKA: Christombu Books, 27 Hospital Street, Colombo 1.
Tel: (01) 433142/328909

TANZANIA: CLC Christian Book Centre, PO Box 1384, Mkwepu Street, Dar es Salaam.
Tel/Fax (022) 2119439

USA: Cook Communications Ministries, PO Box 98, 55 Woodslee Avenue, Paris, Ontario, Canada.
Tel: 1800 263 2664

ZIMBABWE: Word of Life Books, Shop 4, Memorial Building, 35 S Machel Avenue, Harare.
Tel: (04) 781305 Fax: (04) 774739

For email addresses, visit the CWR website: www.cwr.org.uk

CWR is a registered charity – number 294387

Trusted
All Over the World

Daily Devotionals

Books and Videos

Day and Residential Courses

Counselling Training

Biblical Study Courses

Regional Seminars

Ministry to Women

CWR have been providing training and resources for Christians since the 1960s. From our headquarters at Waverley Abbey House we have been serving God's people with a vision to help apply God's Word to everyday life and relationships. The daily devotional *Every Day with Jesus* is read by over three-quarters of a million people in more than 150 countries, and our unique courses in biblical studies and pastoral care are respected all over the world.

For a free brochure about our seminars and courses or a catalogue of CWR resources please contact us at the following address:

CWR,
Waverley Abbey House,
Waverley Lane,
Farnham,
Surrey GU9 8EP
UK

Telephone: +44 (0)1252 784700
Email: mail@cwr.org.uk
Website: www.cwr.org.uk

 CRUSADE FOR WORLD REVIVAL   *Applying God's Word to everyday life and relationships*

The Holy Spirit, Our Counsellor

Focusing on the Holy Spirit, 'the counsellor' who will never leave us, Selwyn Hughes identifies His role in our lives. The Holy Spirit lives in us and brings transformation. A book to encourage us to go straight to Him for our 'counselling' needs as are reminded to open ourselves to the power and working of the Holy Spirit.

£6.99 (plus p&p)

ISBN: 1-85345-309-9

Prayer – A Fresh Vision

Prayer is our pathway to intimacy with the Father – without it we simply cannot grow. If we want to know God and draw closer to Him, then we need to be in conversation with Him.

Selwyn Hughes looks at the basic building blocks of effective prayer using the greatest example of all – Jesus Christ.

£6.99 (plus p&p)

ISBN: 1-85345-308-0

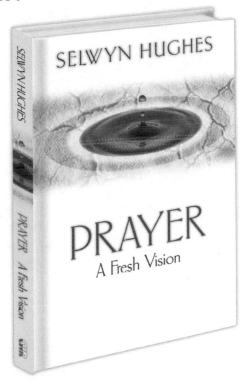

Every Day with Jesus, bimonthly
Selwyn Hughes

One of the most popular daily Bible study tools in the world with nearly three-quarters of a million readers. This inspiring devotional is available bimonthly in regular or large print and as a six-part annual subscription.

£1.99 per issue

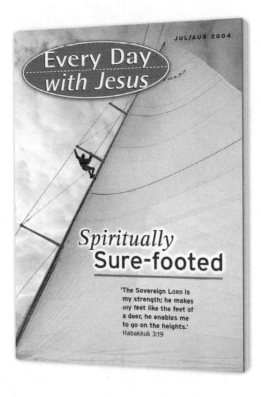